ANCIENT INDONESIA

State of Vermont
Department of Libraries
Midstate Regional Library
RFD 4
Montpelier, Vt. 05602

WITHDRAWN

BY DONALD E. WEATHERBEE

ancient Indonesia

AND ITS INFLUENCE IN MODERN TIMES

—A FIRST BOOK—
Franklin Watts, Inc., New York, 1974

Map by Thomas R. Funderburk
Cover by Terry Fehr

Pictures courtesy of: American Museum of Natural History: 5, 6; Arts et Metiers Graphiques, Paris: 49; Educational Productions, England: 27; Indonesian Tourist Board: 3 (lower), 18, 31 (upper and lower), 32, 55, 57, 60; Information Section, Consulate General, Republic of Indonesia, New York City: 15 (upper), 28, 37, 66, 76 (upper and lower); Illustrated London News: 10; F. Lewis, Publishers, Limited, England: 58; Managing Director of the Indonesia Overseas Bank, Amsterdam: 52; Ministry of Education and Culture of the Republic of Indonesia: 21, 38; Náprstek Museum, Prague: 75; New York Public Library Picture Collection: 41; Oudheidkundige Dienst, Java, 24; Pan American World Airways: 72; United Nations: 3 (upper), 15 (lower), 46 (lower), 63.

Library of Congress Cataloging in Publication Data

Weatherbee, Donald E
    Ancient Indonesia and its influence in modern times.

    (A First book)
    SUMMARY: Examines the effect of Indonesia's ancient history and society on that country's modern civilization.
    Bibliography: p.
    1. Indonesia–History–Juvenile literature. 2. Indonesia–Civilization–Juvenile literature. [1. Indonesia–History. 2. Indonesia–Civilization] I. Title.
DS634.W4   915.98'03   74-3004
ISBN 0-531-02732-5

    Copyright © 1974 by Franklin Watts, Inc.
    Printed in the United States of America
    5 4 3 2 1

CONTENTS

The Indonesian Realm
1

Java Man
4

Old Stone Age
8

The Middle and New Stone Ages
11

Indonesian Metal Workers
16

Indianized States in Indonesia
19

Historical Sources
23

The Central Javanese Period
25

Society in Ancient Java
34

The Kadiri Dynasty
40

The Singasari Dynasty
42

Religious Beliefs
45

The Majapait Empire
47

The Wayang
54

Funeral Practices
59

The Decline of Majapait
and the Coming of Islam
61

The Coming of the Europeans
67

Modern Indonesia
70

Chronology
78

Other Books to Read
79

Index
80

for Mercy Meria Weatherbee
whose first language was Javanese
whose second language was Indonesian

ANCIENT INDONESIA

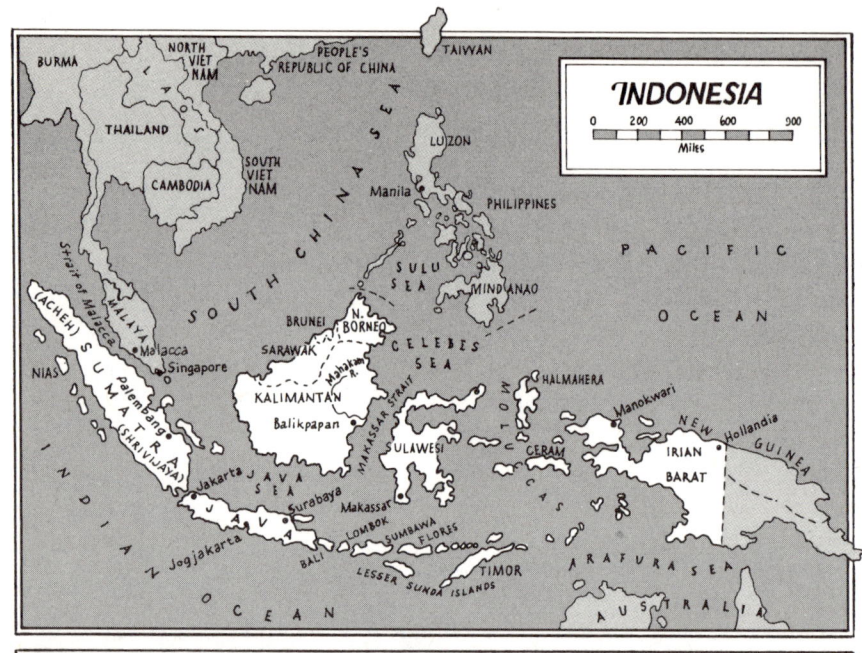
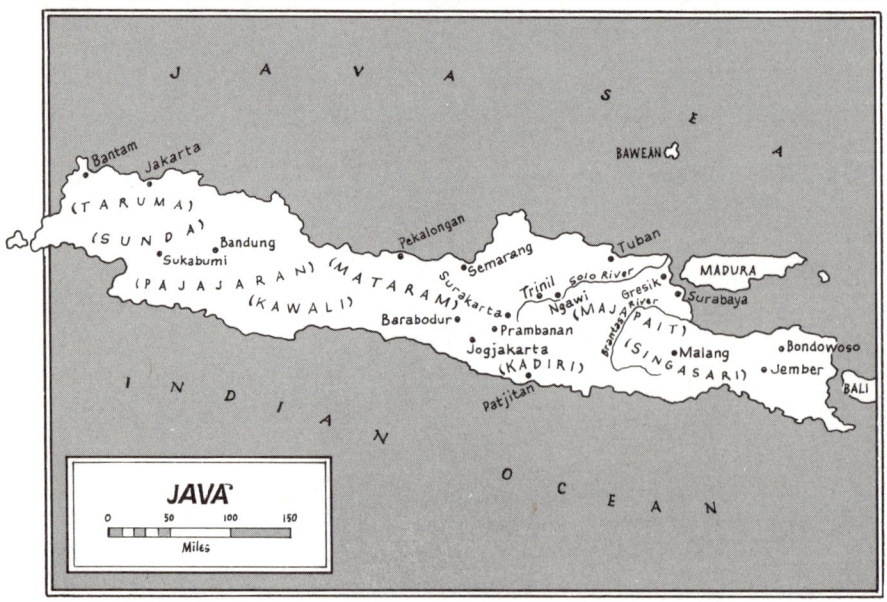

THE INDONESIAN REALM

The emerald necklace of the Indonesian islands arcs from the northern tip of Sumatra to New Guinea in the east, curving northwards through the Moluccas, the fabled Spice Islands, and Sulawesi (Celebes) to the border with the Philippines. Stretching 3,400 miles east to west, the archipelago nation of Indonesia lies astride the equator. There are approximately 3,000 islands in Indonesia, but the five largest make up 90 percent of the land area. *Sumatra* borders the Strait of Malacca, the cockpit of conflict between island empires and mainland power. *Java*, the smallest of the main islands, is the most populous, for more than half of Indonesia's present population of about 125,000,000 lives on it. The recorded history of Indonesia is for a great part the history of Java.

On the north side of the Java Sea Indonesia occupies two-thirds of the giant island of *Kalimantan* (Borneo). The settled part of Kalimantan is along the coastal fringe. The interior remains wild and thinly populated. Octopus-shaped *Sulawesi*, in the east, was thought to be more than one island by early European explorers and was called the Celebes. In 1961–62, the western half of the island of New Guinea, called *Irian Barat* by the Indonesians, became part of the Indonesian nation. Many of the inhabitants of Irian Barat are barely out of the stone age. Mention also should be made of two groups of islands: the Moluccas, the spicey magnets that drew early traders; and the Lesser Sunda islands, anchored at the west by the legendary island of Bali whose culture and arts reflect the heritage of the splendid royal courts of Indonesia's past.

Ancient kingdoms of Java and Sumatra are in parentheses.

The new independent republic of Indonesia came into existence in 1949, when the Dutch, the former colonial rulers, were forced to give up their sovereignty. It is the fifth most populous nation in the world, ranking behind only China, Russia, India, and the United States. Most of the population is engaged in agriculture. In thickly-settled Java and other densely populated localities the basic crop is rice grown in irrigated fields. Indonesia's natural resources in minerals and vegetable products, combined with its population, provides this island country with the potential for becoming a leading Asian nation.

The Indonesian people are scattered among many islands. They represent many different ethnic groups, speak different languages, have different local traditions, and therefore, to help them in the task of building a nation, the leaders of modern Indonesia have appealed to the common background of Indonesian history. Nationalist leaders claim that there is an Indonesian spirit and Indonesian personality, an Indonesian way of doing things that has its roots in the past, although, actually, because of its large population and historical dominance in the archipelago, Javanese culture and civilization is often identified with Indonesian culture and civilization as a whole. The "golden age" of Indonesia's past was the mid-fourteenth century when the great Javanese empire of Majapait culturally and politically dominated the petty courts of the neighboring islands.

Although Indonesian history seems to be clearly marked by the interruptions of successive alien cultural waves and rulers—Indianization, Islamization, Dutch colonialism, the Japanese occupation in World War II, and now Western modernizing ideas—that which is essentially Indonesian continues to give meaning to local life in all its many aspects. Nowhere, naturally, is this more true than on Java itself.

Above: Papuan villagers on the coast of Irian Barat.
Below: Rice fields on the green and fertile island of Bali.

Not only does the study of ancient Indonesian history give us an understanding of what the cultural basis of modern Indonesian society is, it also is important for the study of human society everywhere. Indonesia, and particularly Java, is one of the places in the world where the story of man can be traced in its entirety. Therefore, before we can talk about ancient Indonesian history, we have to discuss prehistory.

JAVA MAN

The history of man as it is set down in words, on paper, metal, clay, or stone covers but a very small fraction of the span of human life on this planet. Man lived and died, worked and loved, for ages before he learned to write. The historian studies man's literary heritage. What does the prehistorian work with? It will depend on his discipline—his special field of knowledge. The palaeontologist studies ancient life on earth through its fossil physical remains: bones, teeth, horn. The archaeologist studies the remains of man's societies through tools, shelters, and household objects. For the historian time passes in years and decades; for the prehistorian, in tens of thousands of years. It is as prehistorians that we begin our look at ancient Indonesia, since there the prehistory of man and his ancestors can be followed back to its earliest stages.

On November 24, 1890, a Dutch palaeontologist, Eugene Dubois, found a fragment of a human-like jawbone among fossil deposits in East Java. A year later Dubois recovered the top of a fossil skull and a tooth of the same species of creature in the dry bed of the Solo River at Trinil in East Java, thirty miles west of the original find. In the fall of 1892, only a few feet from the first Trinil

The Solo River where the fossil bones of the Java ape-man were discovered. Photograph taken in 1894.

find, a leg bone, the left femur, of the same man-like creature was picked up. After examining these bones (the tooth was eventually discarded as not belonging to the skull and femur), Dubois concluded that he had the remains of an ape-man, an ancestor of true man, who could stand upright and had a larger mental capacity than the great apes. Dubois gave his Java ape-man the technical name of *Pithecanthropus erectus* (standing ape-man). Since then, three other examples of *Pithecanthropus erectus* (also called *Homo erectus*) have been found in Java.

Dubois's discovery was a sensation and a triumph of an idea. The scientist had gone to Indonesia from Holland for the express purpose of finding the "missing link" between man and apes; a search which had been intellectually set in motion by the 1859 publication of Charles Darwin's famous *Origin of Species,* the book whose theory of evolution revolutionized man's study of man. Dubois is honored today by a simple monument overlooking the Solo River at Trinil. Beneath this memorial to the discoverer of ancient man in Java, visitors still can pick up stray and casual finds of animal fossils, the stoney tokens of a flourishing jungle life of eons ago.

What kind of people were these early men and near—or not quite—men and how long ago did they live? The palaeontologist thinks of time as measured in terms of long eras of geological and climate changes. We live in the Holocene, or Recent, epoch; the last great epoch before ours began a million years ago—it is called the Pleistocene. The Pleistocene period was marked by the ebb and flow of the huge glaciers, during which time man emerged (more than a million years ago in Africa) and developed. Dubois's discovery was the first of a series of discoveries which proved that Java is one of the places where man has *lived* continuously. Man (and other mammals) did not originate on Java; he crossed from the Asian continent on the land bridges which have since disap-

A modern painting of Java ape-men with a giant tortoise.

peared. But by the happy coincidence of volcanic deposits which had preserved the remains and a very thorough geological survey during the colonial times, an unsurpassed record of man's evolution has been uncovered on this island.

The earliest man-like (*hominid*) creatures on Java, called Old Java Man (*Palaeojavanicus*) combined features of both man and the great ape. He was larger than the modern gorilla. His nearest relatives are to be found among the early pithecanthropid (ape-man) of South and East Africa. *Pithecanthropus erectus*, however, who appeared in the late, middle Pleistocene, was but one variety of a hominid species scattered from North China (Peking Man), to North Africa and even Europe (Heidelberg Man). Although not yet evolved to modern man (*Homo sapiens*), Java Man and his relatives were primitive tool users and, like the Peking Man, may have tamed fire.

OLD STONE AGE

With the appearance of tools we can begin to use the archaeologists' calendar which dates man's progress by his tools and other cultural property. It is close to the boundary between the middle and late Pleistocene that we find the beginnings of tool making: the simple, crude, unspecialized stone implements of the Old Stone Age (Palaeolithic period). The archaeologist calls a particular variety of tools an "industry" and names it after the geographical location where it was first discovered or was most developed. On Java the earliest Palaeolithic industry is called Patjitanian, Patjitan being the place in South Central Java where it was found. Patjitan tools are very rough stone choppers made by flaking away both sides of a core stone. The Patjitan industry is related to a much wider chopping-tool tradition in Asia; the common features of these Asian implements may be because the makers were all from the family of *Pithecanthropus erectus*.

Java ape-man lived in an environment that was cooler and even damper than today's equatorial climate. The land was unsteadied by earthquakes and volcanic activity. The coastline changed as the seas rose and fell with the progress of the glaciers, uncovering and recovering land bridges to mainland Southeast Asia across which the various species of mammals reached what are now islands. Java Man roamed the jungle with primitive elephants, rhinoceros, hippopotamus, bears, tigers, and other predators. He was not very tall. His forehead sloped back in an ape-like way with a heavy beetling brow above his eyes. He had powerful jaws and his teeth were larger than those of modern man. Although it is not known if he had the gift of speech, he was still more man than ape: he thought and he made tools. He and his counterparts elsewhere were the ancestors of *Homo sapiens*.

Sometime in the late Pleistocene, about one hundred thousand years ago, a new species of man arrived in Java. His remains have been found on the banks of the Solo River near Ngawi in East Java. Called Solo Man, he is technically known as *Homo solonensis*. The site where the bones of at least eleven individuals were found may have been a camp ground. Physically Solo Man has much in common with his pithecanthropid ancestors, being closer to his ape-like forebears than to modern man. He had some features in common with the better known Neanderthal Man of Europe. Solo Man possessed an Old Stone Age culture marked by tools made of chipped stones used as scrapers, blades, awls, cleavers, etc. He also used sharpened bones and deer antlers. He was a cannibal, a taste he may have shared with Java Man.

The remains of the first "modern" man (*Homo sapiens*) discovered in Java are known from only two skulls. Wadjak Man, as he

is called, may have been late Pleistocene, but because of the absence of other evidence, little more can be said about him. Palaeolithic tools have been discovered in Sulawesi, which, although human remains have not yet been found with them, may be proof of early migrations from the North, and the Philippines. Some tool finds in Borneo and Sumatra have tentatively been placed in the late Pleistocene.

It is important to remember that as we discuss prehistoric man and his tools, we are limited to those items which were made of durable materials such as stone or fossilized bone. Although palaeolithic man almost surely used wood for such things as clubs, spear shafts, and axe handles, and other vegetable matter for thongs, the traces of these non-permanent materials have disappeared. It would be wrong, therefore, to think of man in the "Stone Ages" being limited to only the use of stone. That which made the "Stone Ages" stone ages is the absence of metal tools.

THE MIDDLE AND NEW STONE AGES

Sometime after the end of the last glacial period, when the islands of Indonesia had finally assumed the forms that we know now, new groups of immigrants began arriving, bringing with them what can be called a Middle Stone Age (Mesolithic) culture. Perhaps

Prehistoric tools such as these are present throughout Indonesia.
Hoes, probably for digging roots and tubers,
are made of deer antlers; the spatula-type tools are of bone.

even before 10,000 B.C., these peoples, the ancestors of the Melanesians and Papuans who live today in New Guinea and the Pacific Islands, crossed the straits on crude rafts, depending on tide and currents to bring them safely ashore. Mesolithic man in Indonesia was a hunter, fisher, and food gatherer. He lived in small groups, perhaps a family cluster, seeking shelter in caves or under rock overhangs. He too was a cannibal, probably no longer simply for food but because the cannibalism had already become connected to the general primitive belief that magic strength could be gained by eating the flesh or vital organs of a strong leader or enemy. The Mesolithic people of Indonesia also shared in a widespread custom of using haematite, red iron oxide, as a mineral paint to imitate blood on the body or bones of the dead and wore human bones as magical charms or amulets. In each of these practices, grisly though they may be, we may see the beginning of religion. (The practices of cannibalism and the staining of the dead with a red substance existed right up to this century among the more remote people of the archipelago.)

There were two, possibly three, separate though inter-mixed tool industries in Mesolithic Indonesia. One, the Hoabinhian, is known especially from sites on the north coast of Sumatra, although the culture is named for a province in North Vietnam where the first site was discovered. On Sumatra the principal tool was a hand-axe made by flaking away a pebble on one side only. This is called a Sumatralith. The Hoabinhian sites on Sumatra are to be found near huge piles of shell-fish refuse, called kitchen middens. On mainland Southeast Asia the beginnings of agriculture and the domestication of animals took place among people who used Hoabinhian tools. This cannot be traced in Indonesia, except, perhaps, for the domestication of the dog.

On Java the best known Mesolithic culture is bone industry. The tools are fishhooks, arrowheads, spear points, awls, scrapers, digging sticks, and daggers made from bone and antler. In South Sulawesi there was a flake and blade culture called Toalean. This survived into historical times and is marked by small-sized stone tools (microliths) for hunting and fishing. It is on the cave walls of these Toalean people that we find the first examples of art in Indonesia. Apparently done for magical purposes, there are a number of hand-stencils, made by spreading the hand, usually the left, against the wall and splashing or painting on red mineral coloring, leaving a negative stencil of the hand on the wall. There is also a wall painting of what looks like a wild pig with a spear point where his heart is located. This is possibly an example of sympathetic magic whereby the painter hoped to guarantee his success as a hunter.

The Mesolithic Age in Indonesia shades into the New Stone Age (Neolithic) without a clear boundary. By at least 3,000 B.C. Neolithic peoples on mainland Southeast Asia had created settled communities based on agriculture supplemented by hunting and fishing. With agriculture came population increase and technical change. Probably by this time the outrigger canoe had been invented. This made it possible for larger groups carrying more goods to travel farther. By 2,000–1,500 B.C. Neolithic peoples were settled throughout the archipelago. Their culture was similar to a widespread culture of mainland Southeast Asia whose principal tool is called the quadrangular adze. This is a hand chisel or gouging tool with a square cross-section. It had a single cutting edge and the whole tool was finished and often highly polished. The quadrangular adze people also made pottery vessels by building up the clay pot by hand; the potter's wheel was not known to them. They made clothes from bark fabric made by beating the bark, after it had been boiled, with a special stone tool, a technique that survived up to this century. They had domesticated the dog and pig, and perhaps even cattle. Their agricultural technique was simple but wasteful. The Neolithic farmers would set fire to a wooded area. After the fire had burned out they would clear the ground for planting. They used digging sticks to open the soil for seed. The same land would be used year after year until its fertility was exhausted. Then the whole village would move on to a new, unused area and the cycle of cutting and burning would begin again. Although this kind of farming leads to smaller and smaller crops over the years and lays the land open to erosion, so long as the population remains fairly small the food requirements of the village can be satisfied. This kind of farming, called swidden agriculture, is still practiced throughout the less populated areas of the outer islands of Indonesia. Its great limitation, other than the fact it can support only a relatively small number of people, is that the crop yield is adequate only for basic needs of life and cannot support a more specialized or highly organized community beyond the farming unit itself. It is not until we are on the very edge of history, that is, the appearance of Indonesians in written records, that we find agricultural methods that support a complex society: the introduction of "wet" (irrigated) rice. In Indonesia this advance was paralleled by a change in the material culture which was perhaps the most significant breakthrough since ape-man on Java had chipped his first rough stone tool; that is, the use of metal.

Before we turn to the metal revolution in ancient Indonesia, however, we should point out that in many areas the Stone Ages still persist today. The idea of a Stone Age is not based on the calendar. There is no automatic progression from one technology to another for a whole region at a given point in time. Side by side with atomic energy, solid-state electronics, and the other elements of modern society the Stone Age co-exists; for example, in New Guinea, among the aborigines of Australia, along the upper Amazon in South America. The Stone Age is a cultural concept and as we continue to look at ancient Indonesia we shall see how older cultural ideas and objects maintain their strength and inner vitality even as newer forms and techniques are grafted on. Development in the Indonesian archipelago was uneven. Java, more than any of the other islands, experienced the impact of great change leading to a highly complex civilization with remarkable cultural achieve-

Above: A mountainous area of Indonesia where primitive farming is still practiced. Below: The Stone Age inhabitants of the mountains of Irian Barat.

ments to its credit. One of the reasons for this is that Java was blessed with the rich soil and ample water supply that made it possible to support a great civilization agriculturally.

INDONESIAN METAL WORKERS

Some time around 500 B.C. a new group of people appear in the archipelago, bringing with them tools and techniques and a complex of beliefs and practices that foreshadow later Indonesian civilization. Moving from a mainland Southeast Asian home land the Malayo-Polynesian immigrants brought a culture and a language that linked the archipelago to a wider sphere. These ancestors of the modern Malay people of Indonesia had tools and weapons of iron and bronze. With an agriculture based on the cultivation of irrigated rice, we can imagine the beginnings of settled village communities perhaps linked together in wider territorial complexes by war chiefs or for special religious ceremonies. In general, the Bronze Age culture of Indonesia is called the Dongson, after the place in coastal central Vietnam where it was recognized as a separate tradition. Two of the most interesting Dongson bronze objects are the ceremonial axes and kettle drums. The large and graceful bronze axe heads could only have had a ritual purpose since they were too fragile and costly for everyday use. They may have belonged to an emerging class of nobles and chieftains as marks of rank, or perhaps they were destined to accompany the souls of the warrior dead into the spirit world. The bronze kettle drums were highly decorated with the drum heads incised with star designs, concentric circles, tangents, flying birds, feathered human forms, buildings, boats, and other figures. The places where such drums have been discovered are distributed throughout Southeast Asia and, in fact, the drums continue to be made by tribal people in Burma and Laos today. The smaller ones may have been war drums while the larger ones probably played a part in the developing religious cult of ancestor worship.

Bronze drums and ceremonial axes have been found on Sumatra, Java, Bali, in the Lesser Sundas, and East Indonesia. The designs and decorations have been preserved in the artistic motifs of contemporary Indonesian groups such as the Toradja people of Central Sulawesi and the Dayaks of Kalimantan. Probably many of the wood and textile designs of the Indonesian peoples of historical times can be traced back to prehistoric ritual symbols and patterns. The magical awe in which the Indonesians held these sacred bronze objects continued right up to the Dutch colonial time. Bronze axes and daggers were believed to be magic "thunder bolts."

The village structure which developed among the new permanent settlements was the origin of the later villages of historical Indonesia. What gave them special meaning—beyond just a territorial one—was the magical/spiritual bond which tied the people together. They were linked both to the past by their ancestors and to daily life with each other by the supernatural forces of nature. Large standing stones or menhirs were thought to be the point of contact between the real world and the world of spirits. The use of large stones in the building of tombs, ceremonial avenues, and as representations of dead ancestors gives us the term megalithic (big-stoned) to describe the practices. On the edge of history then, we can say that Bronze-Iron Age Indonesia was a group of communities of wet-rice growing villagers whose society was already becoming status-divided between commoners, warrior chiefs or princes, and priestly magicians (shamans). Religious belief was centered around the ancestors and animistic notions about nature. Already there was

The soaring houses of the Toradja of Central Sulawesi preserve ancient artistic motifs.

a monumental megalithic architecture. The Indonesians possessed all of the basic elements of their culture when they made the first contacts with the bearers of new cultural ideas from the more highly developed civilization of India.

INDIANIZED STATES IN INDONESIA

The written record of events in Indonesia, the beginning of its history proper, takes place in one of the more remote areas of the archipelago, upstream on the Mahakam River in Kutei, East Kalimantan (East Borneo). There, some fifteen hundred years ago a king named Mulavarman carried out Hindu sacrifices which he commemorated in inscriptions composed in Sanskrit, the language of the Indian religion. Mulavarman was one of the first "Indianized" rulers of Indonesia. By Indianized we mean that although he was an Indonesian he had adopted for official purposes a proper Indian name and had allowed the Brahmans, the priestly class of the Hindu religion, to organize his government. It is likely that Mulavarman's own father was simply a local Indonesian chief. Mulavarman may have adopted Hinduism in order to strengthen himself against rivals competing for Indian trade.

At about the same time as Mulavarman, around A.D. 450, a king named Purnavarman ruled a country called Taruma, situated in the vicinity of modern Jakarta, in West Java. Purnavarman is the first known Indianized ruler from Java. He was a follower of the Hindu god Vishnu. The few inscriptions from his reign reveal that he was a warrior king. His most notable achievement was the construction of a long canal, which shows that even at this very early time Indonesian rulers were concerned with water resources. Taruma's independent existence was probably ended by the aggressive expansion of the Southeast Sumatran state of Shrivijaya.

Shrivijaya emerges in the seventh century. The state was centered in the neighborhood of the modern Palembang on Sumatra. Its prosperity was founded on control of commerce originating in the region around and passing through the Strait of Malacca. Over the centuries Shrivijaya competed for political and military supremacy in the western end of the archipelago, at times holding sway over West Java and the Malay Peninsula. From the earliest days of sea-borne trade, the Straits region was the focus of active international exchange with goods passing to and from China and India and being transhipped from eastern islands. The cargos were mixed: partly luxury items such as sweet smelling woods and resins, spices, medicinal herbs, rare birds and animals, as well as more prosaic items like textiles, grain, and pottery. For a long time people thought that the Indonesian role in this commerce was merely passive and mercantile; now it has been shown that Indonesian ships and sailors shared actively in the trade. Shrivijaya's strategic position and maritime policy guaranteed its material welfare until, in the eleventh century, its power was curbed by stronger enemies. Although there is no distinct Shrivijaya civilization or culture to compare to that of Java, there is enough material and literary remains to prove that the kingdom was a center for Buddhism. Pilgrims would call on their way between India and China. One of the most famous Chinese pilgrims, I Tsing, left a record describing the warm welcome that many Buddhist scholars, at the end of the seventh century, received from the king of Shrivijaya.

An edict carved in stone over a thousand years ago describes the foundation of a royal bathing place on the bank of a Bali river.

One of the major differences between the development of Shrivijaya and later courts of Java with whom they came into conflict was that Shrivijaya was outward looking and the Javanese dynasties inward. Shrivijaya lived on the profits of international trade and was beset on all sides by competition and conflict that often verged on piracy. It did not control large material resources of its own. The Javanese courts on the other hand had a more enduring foundation in agriculture. The ability of the Javanese court to control stocks of rice meant that they could raise armies and large labor forces, support an elaborate bureaucracy, and afford creative artists.

How was the process of the Indianization of local Indonesian rulers accomplished? At first historians thought Indian influences resulted from large scale Indian colonization. It was imagined that waves of immigrants from India settled in Southeast Asia and in the archipelago bringing with them the forms of their own civilization. The vision was of ethnic Indians creating their own courts and, by use of force and cultural superiority, extending their rule over the native inhabitants. If this were true Indonesian history would simply be an extension of Indian history. This colonial vision is no longer accepted, except perhaps for a few Indian "cultural imperialists." It is much more probable that Indian influence was gradually spread by sailors, merchants, and men of religion who traveled through the islands, as far as Sulawesi and as far north as Mindanao in the Philippines. Probably the flow of traffic and ideas was two-way: Indians calling at the coastal points along Sumatra and Java; Indonesians marveling in India at the accomplishments of that civilization.

One can imagine a local chief on Java or Sumatra, engaged in trade with the foreign trader, coming into contact not only with his business practices but also with his Indian culture and religion. The Indonesian sought in the new ideas and rituals support for his local status and position while the Indian wished to further his own economic or religious interests. Very likely, the Indians, culturally sure of themselves, buttressed their preferred status through marriage with the daughters of the local chiefs. Probably the first Indianized Indonesian rulers hoped for, from the foreigner with his new form of ritual magic, an ally against local competition.

The process of Indianization must have taken several centuries, but gradually it gave new form to government, religion, and art. It did not however penetrate or transform the foundations of Indonesian society, particularly that of Java where the greatest cultural achievements of Indonesia were made.

HISTORICAL SOURCES

Before tracing the accomplishments of the Javanese it is proper to explain what sources we have for reconstructing the past. In the first place there are inscriptions on stone and copper—official records of land grants, legal decisions, special privileges, etc. Royal inscriptions were treated as holy objects. Most of them are written in Old Javanese, the language of the people, as opposed to Sanskrit, the language of the court religions. These original inscriptions are the raw material of history, as are literary remains of court poetry and prose that have been saved through the centuries by faithful copying. Pious Balinese, whose culture is still Indianized, transcribed many of these works such as the *Ramayana* and the *Bharatayuddha* from their Sanskrit originals although the scenes take place in a Javanese landscape. Religious texts give us an idea of their rules and doctrines of belief. There are some later, fifteenth and sixteenth century traditions of East Javanese dynastic history, again preserved through the intermediary of the Balinese copyist; while a long court poem from the middle of the fourteenth cen-

tury called the *Nagarakertagama* gives a vivid and detailed picture of life at the Javanese court at the height of the Majapait period, when the East Java power was dominant in the archipelago, its sway extending to the Peninsula Southeast Asia as well.

Supplementing the written record is the wealth of archaeological finds from ancient Java. Since almost all structures for everyday use in ancient Java were built of perishable materials such as bamboo and thatch, the buildings which remain, of stone and brick, are of special significance. They are called *candis* and most of them are either Buddhist or Shivaite religious sanctuaries, which at the same time were tombs for the noble dead. In addition to the buildings there are stone images of Hindu and Buddhist gods. Some of these images are portraits of dead kings and queens who are thought to be identified with the particular god.

THE CENTRAL JAVANESE PERIOD

The first dated inscription from Central Java tells us that in the year A.D. 732 a king named Sanjaya erected for the welfare of his subjects a *linga* with all of the signs of good fortune. The *linga* is the most common image representing the Hindu high god Shiva in his creative aspect. Sanjaya was considered by his descendants to be the founder of the Mataram dynasty. Sanjaya probably was a first-generation Indianized Indonesian ruler, for his father had an

A sculpted relief showing a scene from the Ramayana.

Indonesian name. The princes of the Mataram dynasty through two hundred years were ardent followers of Shiva.

The slopes and plains of Central Java are dotted with the remains of the Shivaite temples constructed during this period. Shiva was a god who could be gentle or cruel, beautiful or demonic. He was the supreme god among the three main Hindu deities—Brahma, Shiva, and Vishnu. The Indonesians were able to associate the worship of Shiva with their old, deeper attachment to ancestor worship and native gods of the mountains. The Shivaite temples or *candis* are for the most part of simple construction. Built of stone they had three parts: a basement, a room for the main image, and a roof. Inside the main part of the temple there was an image of the god Shiva in one of his forms, most often as a statue known as a *linga*. In niches on the side walls stood images of the deities most closely associated with him: his wife, Parvati; his elephant-headed son, Ganesha; and the ancient pot-bellied holy man, Agastya. On the temple grounds there often was placed an image of Shiva's mount, the bull Nandi. Since the Javanese did not use the arch in their building, the walls and roofs of these temples were massively constructed. The Shivaite and Buddhist monuments of Java should not be thought of as churches. People did not enter them to worship. Those who attended the ceremonies at the sanctuary gathered outside. Only the chief priest and one or two of his attendants approached the image of the god inside, to anoint it with the holy water.

Shiva was not the only high-god worshipped in Central Java. Simultaneously with the Shivaite kings of Sanjaya's dynasty another royal family, that of the Shailendras, the "Kings of the Mountain," professed Mahayana Buddhism which found expression in some of the grandest Buddhist architecture to be found in the world. It is

The marriage of Shiva and Parvati, a stone relief from India that is thought to have influenced Indonesian art of the time.

not clear what the origins of the Shailendra dynasty were (perhaps refugees from the old Cambodian empire of Funan) or exactly what relationship they had with the Sanjaya kings with whom they coexisted. By the middle of the ninth century under a Sanjaya king, Pikatan, the families may have been united through Pikatan's marriage with the daughter of the last Javanese Shailendra ruler. The Shailendra also ruled in Shrivijaya, perhaps driven there by the forces of Shivaite reaction.

It would be wrong to think of the relationship between Buddhism and Shivaism on Java as simply one of antagonism. The Northern (Mahayana) Buddhism which the Shailendra kings professed was closer to Shivaism than it was to original Buddhist thought. The Mahayanists had developed a very complicated system of gods each of which eventually became associated with its Shivaite counterpart. By the thirteenth century in East Java there was little difference between Buddha and Shiva.

One thing is clear: The archaeological remains in central Java demonstrate that the rulers had the capability to put together the resources, material and human, to carry out large scale building enterprises. The epitome of the Mahayanist aspiration to realize in stone the symbols and logic of the religious system is the world-famous Barabodur. It is one of the most remarkable religious monuments ever built. The building consists of nine stone terraces spiraling up a natural hill. Each terrace has a walled gallery around it and on the walls are carved, in high relief, nearly a mile and a half of panels depicting Buddhist legends. As the pilgrim toured the terraces, moving in a clock-wise fashion, he also moved, ideally at least, through the stages of the Buddhist universe, until he approached the images set on the upper terraces which depicted the complicated system of the particular Buddhist gods to which

A gigantic statue of Buddha, believed to have been erected by the same splendor-loving king who ordered Barabodur built.

Barabodur was dedicated, the "Bearers of the Thunderbolt." At the top was the *dagob*, a bell-shaped enclosure which concealed the image of the Adi-Buddha, the source of all else. The Barabodur was an earthly replica of the Buddhist cosmos and at the same time it was probably the tomb of a Shailendra king. While the conception of the Barabodur is a magnificent example of the translation of religious speculation to art, the actual task of construction was staggering. Some idea of the immensity of the task is conveyed by the fact that it required two million cubic feet of stone. One can hardly imagine the labor required to move this stone with primitive equipment. Its construction, in addition, must have required hundreds of stone cutters, sculptors, and artists. And all of these people had to be fed by other people.

In the thousand years since its erection Barabodur has fallen into disrepair through neglect, bad drainage, the growth of lichens, and other ravages of time. A few years ago it became apparent that it was in immediate danger of collapse. In order to save Barabodur, a major international rescue effort has been mounted through UNESCO to provide financial assistance and expertise to the Indonesian government. It will be dismantled, stone by stone, and rebuilt.

The largest and most splendid Shivaite monument on Java is the temple complex of Prambanan, between the modern cities of Jogjakarta and Solo in South Central Java. Probably Pikatan was enshrined here in the second half of the ninth century. The central monument at Prambanan is a towering Shiva temple. It is flanked by temples dedicated to Vishnu and Brahma, the other gods of the classic Hindu trinity. In a splendid example of the application of

*Above: The Buddhist monument of Barabodur with its magnificent sculptures and reliefs.
Below: One of the series of stone carvings from the terraces of Barabodur.*

modern archaeological and architectural techniques by two generations of devoted Dutch and Indonesian engineers, draftsmen, and laborers, the central temple has been restored to its former greatness. Not the least of Prambanan's wonders are the impressive panels of the gallery running around the base of the tower on which scenes from the famous epic, the *Ramayana*, are carved. In one of the stanzas of a tenth-century Javanese version of the *Ramayana*, a temple complex which may be Prambanan itself is described in detail.

In the first half of the tenth century the seat of power shifted to East Java, in the valleys of the Solo and Brantas rivers. From at least A.D. 926 on, the date of the first inscription of King Sindok, the Javanese court was East Javanese. This does not mean that East Java was colonized from Central Java. The earliest inscription from East Java, dated A.D. 760, proves the existence of an Indianized court in the Malang region. A half-century later, religious officials were regulating irrigation works on a tributary of the Brantas river. (After Sindok, Central Java does not again emerge as an important political or cultural center until Islamic times.) A number of suggestions have been made to explain the transfer of the *kraton* (court). According to Sindok's inscriptions his was not a peaceful time. It is possible that internal strife coinciding with conflict with Shrivijaya may have led to a withdrawal toward the east. It is also possible that natural disasters, earthquakes, and volcanic eruptions brought ruin to Middle Java. Another theory is that the overwhelming demands on the population by the temple builders were too much; that people began to move away to escape being used as forced labor on these shrines and thus gradual depopulation took place. Be that as it may, it is clear that the pattern of life in the Indianized Java had been set for the future.

The Prambanan temple complex has been restored to its ancient grandeur.

SOCIETY IN ANCIENT JAVA

At the summit of the social structure was the king. He was titled *Shri Maharaja,* a Sanskrit rank of nobility. He also had an Indonesian title which came to mean king: *ratu.* Below him were a number of nobles who apparently had certain rights over land. Their title was *rakaryan* or *pamgat,* both terms being of Indonesian origin. There were numerous lesser officials who bore titles denoting their functions, but unfortunately, we do not know exactly what the terms mean. The clergy was organized in a bureaucracy that paralleled and suggested the organization of the nobility. In the lower ranks of the secular administration were officials called *patihs* who linked the royal sphere to the village sphere.

Indonesian villages remained relatively unchanged through the centuries. The population was divided on the basis of age and sex. Government in the villages was in the hands of elders. Each village had elders in charge of particular activities: irrigation, hunting, forestry, calendar-keeping, etc. In the wet-rice culture which developed, the organizing principle of village life was cooperation for the common good. The connection between village and the noble courts was made when the courts needed taxes in the form of rice deliveries or labor for the building of monuments. Between the courts and the villages existed another group of the population involved in arts, crafts, music, magic, etc. These were people who had special skills serving a community wider than the villages: dyemakers, potters, lime burners, basket weavers, carpenters, iron smiths, foreign traders, masked dancers, minstrels, etc. They lived on the "king's dues" and seemed to have certain special privileges. These privileges may have in part been a result of a belief in the magically dangerous nature of their vocations, going back to prehistoric traditions.

It has been suggested that there was a clear boundary between court and village defined by the cultural attachments of the two: the royal court being Indianized; the village remaining basically Indonesian. This view which tends to place ruler and realm into an antagonistic cultural relationship is contradicted by the view from the vantage point at which this writer stands to observe the panorama of ancient Javanese history. Although the texts left to us by the Brahmanic clerks of the royal courts depict a thoroughly Indianized society, it is more likely that the orthodoxy was more verbal than real. Despite the trappings of an Indian religion and law that surrounded and philosophically underpinned them, the courts remained essentially Indonesian. This is substantiated by the fact that the most important organizing principle of Indian society, the institution of caste, was not transferred to Indonesia as a social reality. Contrary to the view that Indonesian society was split into ruler and realm on the basis of values transported from India, there is a school of thought that holds that Indianization was but a thin veneer over an Indonesian foundation; that it did not bring any fundamental changes to Indonesian social and political order. This does not deny the tremendous impact of Indian art and ideas, rather, it emphasizes the processes by which these ideas and cultural forms became absorbed in the Indonesian cultural sphere and stresses the persistence of the local tradition as the basic framework of human life in ancient Indonesia.

For an example, let us take a close look at how one of the most common royal official acts in ancient Java was carried out. Of all the inscriptions that we have, by far the largest number refer to the granting of rights to land. Although the ancient Javanese king did not own all the land, he did possess certain rights in the disposal of its products through taxes and gifts. Very often the king was called upon to give up these rights and to set land free for the benefit of a religious shrine, not uncommonly a tomb. This donation of land was called a *sima*. The inscriptions in the old Javanese language give a different and probably more accurate picture of the Indonesian society than the more emotional output of the court poets and clerks.

The core of the rite at the *sima* took place around a stone placed on a terrace in the midst of the sacred ground; the stone was called the *watu kulumpang*, a purely Indonesian name. The rite was conducted by the *hyang kudur*, a non-Brahmanic religious official whose duties may have been related to ancient shamanistic practices. During the ceremony those present were grouped around the stone: in the north, the representatives of royal authority, officials and nobles; in the west, the *hyang kudur* and his attendants, in the south the local villagers. The space to the east probably was usually empty, reserved perhaps for the gods and spirits invoked by the *hyang kudur* to be present at the scene. These gods not only included a strange assortment of major and minor Hindu deities, but also animistic spirits of local and natural forces. A variety of objects were offered to the *watu kulumpang*, including tools and other utensils employed in the preparation of the sacrifice, and which therefore had acquired so much magical power human beings no longer could use them. The critical moment in the establishment of the *sima* came when the *hyang kudur* killed a chicken, dripped its blood over the stone, and laid a terrible, blood curdling curse against anyone who in the future might violate the rights granted over the land. This ceremony around the *watu kulumpang* is in its origin Indonesian, not Indian. It bound the villager and the representatives of the court together in a rite that linked them to their own, megalithic past. The ceremony of the confirmation of the *sima* ended with all of the participants having

Scenes from a Balinese epic showing ancient court life.

a meal together while performances of magical religious dances and masked plays took place. This common meal shows the social unity of early Indonesian society. There is no hint of the prohibitions of caste. In this communal feast, when the community marked an important sacred event, we probably have the ancestor of the modern Javanese *slametan:* a communal meal which links the individual to the wider community, past and future.

The purpose of the *sima*, or land grant, gives us another example of the way in which the traditional Indonesian background penetrated the Indian veneer. Most often the products of the *sima* were to be used to support a religious shrine called a *dharma* (although all remains are now called indiscriminately *candi*). The *dharma* had a temple dedicated to a particular god from the Shivaite or Buddhist pantheon. The image of this god was the central focus of the temple. At the same time that the god was being worshipped in an orthodox manner, royal ancestors were being honored since it was the practice to enshrine the noble dead in a way in which their souls were thought of as being united with the god in an image. In this way a magical link was established between the ruler and his royal predecessors and dynastic power flowed from a magical-religious, supernatural source. Ancestor worship, although not on such a grand scale, was practiced by the common people as well in family shrines. The founders of the village were venerated in community shrines. In the cult of dead royalty the image of the Indian god became part of Indonesian ancestor worship. In the later Singasari and Majapait dynasties the royal dead were united with gods in so-called portrait statues; that is an image of the god having the features of the person to be enshrined.

A modern slametan or communal meal.

THE KADIRI DYNASTY

After Sindok, there is a lack of documentary sources in East Java until we reach the eleventh century. In 1016–17, the royal city of the King Dharmawangsa Teguh was overrun by an invading force that probably had connections with Shrivijaya. This was in retaliation for an attack that Teguh had made on Shrivijaya. All of East Java was thrown into turmoil. It was a number of years before Teguh's son-in-law, the half-Balinese Airlangga, was able to restore central authority. Airlangga's mother was Sindok's grand-daughter and married to a Balinese prince. Bali enters history with an inscription dated A.D. 823 and written in old Balinese. Already Bali had a structure of Indianized courts not dissimilar to Java's. Undoubtedly cultural exchanges had taken place very early in the history of East Java and Bali. Since Airlangga, Balinese and Javanese history has been tied together with Bali being in a dependent position.

After centralizing authority on Java, Airlangga, strangely enough, divided his kingdom between his sons. This may have been to prevent a civil war on his death. It was not long, however, before power was again concentrated at one court, Kadiri, in a dynasty that had seven kings (A.D. 1117–1222). The heart of Kadiri was located on the upper reaches of the Brantas River, south of the center of Airlangga's kingdom. The Kadiri kings proclaimed that they were incarnations of Vishnu. In Hindu mythology the god

Rama himself in a Javanese relief of the Ramayana.

Vishnu descends to earth in human form in times of misfortune to restore the world's welfare. The Kadiri kings were patrons of literature and during this period the poetic arts flourished in the form of *kekawins*. A *kekawin* is a particular form of poetry which is composed according to very strict rules of Indian meter. It was court poetry written under the patronage of nobles. Although the poets took as their themes subjects from Sanskrit literature and epics, the settings were purely Javanese. From these poems we can get an idea of what the Javanese countryside was like. The poets glorified their royal benefactors comparing them to Hindu gods in their magnificence. The oldest *kekawin* known, the Old Javanese *Ramayana*, probably dates from the tenth century. It has been suggested that court poetry had a magical function. The court poet was a verbal magician, in this view, weaving a new reality in order to disguise events in the old. An example of this is the *kekawin Arjunawiwaha* (*The Marriage of Arjuna*) which can be interpreted as an allegory on the career of Airlangga. At the same time, however, the Old Javanese poets were interested in the same thing that poets everywhere are: the pursuit of beauty.

THE SINGASARI DYNASTY

The year A.D. 1222 is the date given by Javanese historical sources for the defeat of the last king of Kadiri by Ranggah Rajasa (alias Angrok) the founder of the Singasari dynasty. Rajasa was a vassal of Kadiri ruling over territory to the east of the Kawi and Arjuna mountains. Later tradition viewed Rajasa as the son of the high god Shiva. The greatest of the Singasari kings was Kertanagara. His royal consecration occurred in 1254 and he died in 1292. This period is noteworthy in at least three major respects. In the first place, under Kertanagara's patronage, tantric Buddhism (after *tantra*, the secret texts used by the worshippers) flourished. He himself was consecrated a Buddhist divinity. Secondly, under Kertanagara the Javanese empire in the archipelago began to take shape. Finally his foreign policy brought him into conflict with the new, dynamic Mongol court in China which led to a Mongol invasion of Java.

As an empire builder, Kertanagara first conquered Bali and then, in 1275, he mobilized his forces for a military expedition against the Sumatra kingdom of Malayu. Malayu's submission to Java was demonstrated by its king's acceptance of a copy of the temple image of Kertanagara's father as a symbol of Singasari dynastic power on Sumatra. Furthermore, there is a persistent tradition in the Javanese sources which claims that the Malayu king delivered up two of his daughters to Kertanagara as tribute. Kertanagara's foreign adventures took place in an international environment that saw in China the decline of the Sung dynasty and the victory of the Mongols.

While Kertanagara had extended himself in Sumatra, rebellion occurred at home when Jaya Katwang, a descendant of the Kadiri kings, rose against him. Despite a stout defense by the Singasari forces the troops of Kadiri stormed the court, killed Kertanagara, and sacked and pillaged Singasari. One of Kertanagara's ablest military leaders, his son-in-law Wijaya, was able to escape to Madura, where with the aid of its regent he was able to raise another army. The decisive factor in the struggle was the intervention of a Mongol army in East Java in 1293–1294.

The background to the Mongol invasion of Java has to be set within the framework of the traditional Chinese approach to international relations in the area. It has been remarked that the history of the states of Southeast Asia is in part an extension of the history of China; that is, in periods of dynastic weakness in China strong states could arise in Southeast Asia and in a period of dynastic strength in China, only weak states in Southeast Asia would be tolerated. The Chinese connection with its neighbors was based on inequality. The kings of the smaller neighbor states were expected to acknowledge the Chinese emperor as their elder brother. This recognition of his senior position in the Confucian family of nations was given material substance in the practice of sending tribute missions to the Chinese court. In return the Chinese emperor would officially recognize the Southeast Asian ruler as sovereign in his own land. Javanese kings had been tribute bearers to China from the beginnings of the Indianized states. It is possible that under the disguise of tribute missions we can see international trade, but the symbolic value to the Chinese of the submission of the rulers of the Southeast Asian lands should not be underestimated. When the Mongols under Kubilai Khan, the son of Jenghis Khan, established their regime in China (the Yuan Dynasty, A.D. 1260–1368), they sought to reestablish the traditional pattern of Chinese relations with the south by the use of force. According to the Mongols, their emissary to Kertanagara, requesting him to send tribute, was humiliated and his ears were cut off. To enforce submission, Kubilai ordered an army to be sent. This force landed in East Java in the midst of the civil war between Wijaya, seeking to reestablish the rights of the Rajasa line of kings, and Jaya Katwang, the Kadiri conquerer of Kertanagara. Wijaya and the Mongols joined forces and together defeated the Kadiri armies. Then Wijaya turned on his Mongol allies and expelled them from the island. Wijaya founded a new court at Majapait, the last of the Indianized courts of ancient Java.

RELIGIOUS BELIEFS

Before we turn to the Majapait court we should pause a moment to take a look at the development of religious expression in East Java. As we noted earlier there was, from the beginning, a tendency for the differences between Shivaism and Buddhism to blur. In many ways the two religions became but different aspects of the same way of thinking. From the thirteenth century on the "Shiva-Buddhism" of the royal courts was strongly influenced by the addition of magical rites and practices which sought to unite the individual with the god. This tantric Buddhism was similar to the development of Buddhism in Tibet, which evolved into Lamaism. Central to the religion was the discipline of Yoga. But there were other, easier ways to become joined with the god. The most terrible were cults that worshipped the god as a demon, a Bhairava. One approached the evil aspect of the god through blood sacrifices carried out in drunken stupor in the middle of cemeteries. There are portrait images showing royalty in the form of the demon god, drinking from a skull full of blood, knife in hand, human sacrifice at his feet. Kertanagara himself was a Bhairava worshipper.

Although tantric Buddhism permeated the religious atmosphere of the Singasari and, later, Majapait court society, it is doubtful that it had any great appeal beyond this narrow circle. It too, like Shivaism, did not transform religious thinking in the wider Javanese community.

The religious background of traditional Javanese society was grounded in myths and rituals connected with agricultural fertility and control over the forces of nature. When an Indian high god entered the religious system of the village, it did so in a way which identified it with an indigenous supernatural being or force. For example, the central female divinity in traditional Indonesian myth and religion is a personification of fertile agriculture. In

wet-rice cultures she is the rice goddess, called on Java, Dewi Shri. Throughout the archipelago there are many similarities in the rice or agricultural myths which prove their Indonesian origin. Dewi Shri is worshipped particularly at the time of the rice harvest with special ceremonies and offerings. At the same time, however, Dewi Shri could be brought into the official court pantheon by identifying her with Shri Laksmi, the female partner of Vishnu. The rituals of the traditional religion were not directed to the building of monuments. There is no archaeological record of village shrines. These places of offering, devoted to ancestors, local spirits, the goddess Shri, have perished. It is only in myth and the survival of fragments of rituals such as the *slametan* that we are able to get some insight into it. Javanese villages still practice the annual custom of *bersih desa*, that is, cleansing or purifying the community of evil spirits that might be harboring there.

THE MAJAPAIT EMPIRE

Wijaya was the founder of Majapait in 1294. This kingdom, with its center located on the lower Brantas River, was the greatest of the Indianized courts of Java, although we have decided this because this is the court that we know the most about. In its day

Above: Modern worshippers on the steps of one of the many temples on the island of Bali. Below: Women harvesting rice as they have done for hundreds of years.

Majapait's influence and fame was widespread in Southeast Asia; for later generations of Javanese and Indonesians it represented a kind of golden age. The later Moslem rulers of Java even tried to claim descent from the non-Moslem rulers of Majapait. The Majapait court became the model for other dependent courts in the archipelago. For example, the traditional history of the Sultanate of Kutei, which we already have noted as being the location of the earliest inscriptions from Indonesia, tells us that its first properly consecrated king went to Majapait to learn the correct customs and methods for the organization of his own court. During the height of Majapait's dynastic strength its influence stretched throughout the archipelago. The *Nagarakertagama,* a *kekawin* by a Buddhist priest, Prapanca, which glorifies the Majapait king Rajasanagara (1350–1389), gives a long list of the dependencies of the Majapait court covering most of modern Indonesia and the Malay Peninsula. There is another passage in the *Nagarakertagama* which describes the lively trade carried on by the Majapait ports throughout the whole Asian region. One example of how elements of Javanese culture were dispersed in the Majapait sphere of influence is the spread of the so-called Panji stories.

The Panji cycle of myth and legend has a distinctly Javanese background, probably obtaining its present form during the middle or late Majapait period. The stories tell of the adventures of Panji, a Javanese prince who is an incarnation of Vishnu. Panji is separated from his beloved, a Javanese princess who is an incarnation of the goddess Shri. After innumerable encounters with demons, foreign kings, and other princesses, Panji and Shri are finally reunited, which symbolically means that social unity is once again restored. Panji tales, which became part of the puppet theater repertoire and are depicted in relief on late Majapait *candis,* are encountered not

*Statue of a
Javanese princess.*

only in Javanese tradition, but are also known in Malaya, Thailand, and even as far away as Cambodia.

There is no doubt that Majapait attempted to impose its political will on its two closest neighbors, Bali and Sunda (West Java), by force. Bali was invaded again in 1343 by the Javanese. A Majapait prince was installed as overlord and there was apparently large scale settlement on Bali by a Javanese army of occupation. To this day the ruling class on Bali call themselves "men of Majapait." It was during this time that the final and most thorough Javanizing of Balinese civilization took place. In many ways Balinese culture still reflects aspects of what Majapait must have been like.

Sunda, Majapait's western neighbor on the island of Java itself, had always occupied a precarious position between Javanese power and strong states centered on the Straits region. There is fragmentary evidence that Sunda had been at different times under the control of Shrivijaya and East Javanese courts. In a policy inspired by the Majapait prime minister, Gajah Mada, the Javanese sought to bring Sunda under their sway in the middle of the fourteenth century. This was to be symbolized by the delivery of the Sundanese princess as tribute to the Majapait king, Rajasanagara. The outcome of the scheme was bloodshed and tragedy; the material for one of the most poignant episodes in Javanese literature. It was proposed that a marriage take place between the Sundanese princess and the Javanese ruler. The Sundanese agreed to this, but when they arrived at Majapait for the wedding they were told that it was not a match between equals but that the Princess was a tribute offering. The Sundanese king, unwilling to acknowledge dependency on Majapait, refused to deliver his daughter. A great battle ensued, and in the words of a Javanese history: "The Sundanese were exterminated without exception." This took place in 1357.

The deceptive proposal of marriage and the tragic consequences have been the subject of Javanese poetry in *kidung* form. A *kidung*, as opposed to *kekawin*, is a poem in Indonesian meters using romantic themes drawn from real events. A *kidung* can be compared to the minstrel songs of the European age of chivalry. The earliest Javanese inscriptions prove that there was a class of professional musicians, poets, singers, and dancers, whose function was not just entertainment, but who probably carried out performances that had a sacred ritual meaning as well. One of these early artists was the *mangidung*. One can imagine him as a kind of troubadour, rhyming and singing a tale which once was fact but eventually became a kind of fiction: a *kidung*. The *kidung Sunda* is a good example. We have some idea of the historical facts of the affair. The poem however has turned a political dispute into a tragic romance. The match between the unfortunate princess and the Majapait king is a love match. The Javanese king chose her from all the women in the empire to be his wife. It is only because of the trickery of his advisers who wish to get political advantage that the tribute demand is made. After the death in battle of her father and retainers, the princess commits suicide by throwing herself in the funeral pyre. The Javanese king is left broken-hearted.

It was during the reign of the king, Rajasanagara, that the *Nagarakertagama* was composed. Its purpose was to glorify the splendor of the king and his court. Prapanca, the poet, left us a vivid picture of what life was like at the Majapait court. Occasionally the king ventured from the capital into the countryside. We have a lively impression of such a royal trip. Everyone in the court went. The highway was jammed with the carts of the party, a fourteenth century traffic jam. Around the carts of the nobles and officials crowded hordes of men and women on foot: servants, soldiers, minor officials, hangers-on, the local curious, etc. In and among this human throng moved innumerable horses, elephants, and oxen. It was a colorful scene with the carts painted and decorated in distinctive ways so that the rank and identity of its occupant could be easily recognized. The whole procession would halt late in the afternoon and the local villages would have the honor and burden of hosting the hungry, thirsty mob. When the king went

hunting he and his nobles would stay by their carts while hundreds of servants encircled the woods and by loud cries and the use of dogs would drive the game to the hunters.

Each year in the month of Caitra (March-April) there was a great festival in Majapait. Probably this festival had its roots in older festivals that marked the agricultural calendar. Even later Moslem festivals connected to an Islamic religious calendar contained elements of the Indonesian background. In these festivals there were dances or rituals that seemed to connect the ruler with the rice goddess, Dewi Shri. The culmination of the Caitra festival was a huge meal. At three o'clock in the afternoon the king and his nobles sat down to an immense repast eating mutton, buffalo, poultry, wild game, boar, fish, and duck washed down with a variety of alcoholic beverages: palm wine, rice wine, and other fermented drinks. Apparently everybody indulged very heavily for Prapanca mentions that the liquor flowed like water and many were drunk and sick. The sober members of the party laughed at them. During the course of the party entertainment was presented. Everyone took part; the king himself singing *kidungs* and drinking with the dancing girls. Everything led up to the performance of a masked dance or play called *raket* in which the king took the central part. It may be that the *raket* was the acting out of the central fertility myth of this agricultural society. It is through the legends and myths that make up the repertoire of the traditional theater arts of Java that we are able to get some knowledge about the way in which the ancient Indonesians looked at the world. This is particularly true of the puppet or *wayang* plays.

*A royal procession with
elephants from Barabodur.*

THE WAYANG

The *wayang* or shadow play is the most popular form of drama in Java. For centuries it has been influential in the shaping of Javanese values and attitudes. Although over the years variations of the *wayang* have occurred, basically it is a performance of a play using flat leather puppets. It is called a "shadow play" because between the puppet master (*dalang*), who is also the narrator, and the audience a cotton screen is stretched. The *dalang* manipulates the puppets in front of an oil lamp and on the other side of the screen the audience can see the shadow. This kind of silhouette theater has existed on Java for a thousand years or more. It is thought by some that it had its origin in rituals related to ancestor worship; the shadows of the puppets representing the spirits or ghosts of the ancestors.

The *wayang* stories are drawn from the Javanized Indian epic tales of the *Ramayana* and the *Mahabharata*. Puppets are made in a very stylized fashion to represent the chief characters. On the one side there are forces of good, on the other evil. A central idea expressed in the *wayang* is that both are necessary for universal harmony. The ethics and morality expressed through *wayang* performances has had a profound influence on the Javanese world view.

A modern performance of the *wayang*, which can be specified as *wayang kulit* (leather) to distinguish it from other, later kinds of *wayang* performances, is accompanied by the Javanese orchestra, called *gamelan*. The *gamelan* consists of a variety of gongs and xylophone-like instruments played by striking metal keys with a

The back view of a performance of a wayang, or shadow play, showing the dalang, or puppet master working his puppets.

hammer. It is led by a stringed instrument called a *rebab* played with a bow, like a violin or cello. We know that the Javanese orchestra and the kind of music it plays is Indonesian. Similar instruments and musical scales have been traced as far as the east coast of Africa where ancient Indonesian voyages once touched. The puppet master narrates the story in a sing-song fashion while moving the arms of the puppets which are arranged in front of him, their spines stuck in the stock of a banana branch. The forces of good are traditionally on the right, evil on the left. Occasionally the puppeteer raps a box in front of him to emphasize scene changes. The ritualistic element of a *wayang* performance is now largely lost. People will sit on both sides of the screen, although there usually is segregation by sex and age. A performance begins around 9:00 at night and will continue to dawn. No one, except the puppeteer, pays attention all the time. The audience drifts in and out, eating and drinking. Sometimes the men will play cards or chess. Everyone already knows the story and will turn back to the performance when the exciting or climactic points occur. The Javanese identify personally with different *wayang* characters. One of the popular moments in the plays is when the course of action is interrupted by a character called Semar. Even though the story is one that was originally based on an Indian epic, Semar, a thoroughly Indonesian figure, appears. As in so many other aspects of Javanese life, Semar represents the basic Indonesian foundation under the Indianized veneer.

Other forms of *wayang* also convey traditional values and attitudes to modern audiences. The *wayang gedog* is based on the Panji cycle of stories, which emphasize the chivalric virtues of the noble warrior. *Wayang* performances with human actors, *wayang wong*, are masked dances with the skilled performers suggesting with their bodies the two-dimensional flatness of a puppet. Another *wayang* theater, using three-dimensional wooden puppets, devel-

Gamelan orchestra players in Bali.

A batik sarong decorated with mythical figures from the wayang.

oped taking its repertoire from the adventures of a Moslem hero, Amir Hamza. *Wayang* is even broadcast over the radio in Indonesia today, reaffirming the conclusion that it is not the theater form that is important but the stories. One cannot overestimate the degree to which *wayang* has molded Javanese life.

FUNERAL PRACTICES

We have noticed several times how important the cult of the ancestor was in ancient Indonesia. On Java we have seen how the shrine and the image in it was the point of contact between the living and the dead. In the *Nagarakertagama* there is a description of the ceremony whereby the soul of the ancestor is released from its earthly bonds and goes to paradise. This ceremony was called a *shraddha* and took place twelve years after death. The great *shraddha* that took place in 1362 was for the king's grandmother, Rajapatni, who had been a wife of Rajasa and the daughter of Kertanagara: a very important woman. We should mention here that women held high status in ancient Indonesia. They had rights far beyond their sisters in India. This is another evidence of how little Indianization changed traditional Indonesian society. In fact, there is evidence which shows that rights of inheritance through the mother's line of descent was an important principle.

Rajapatni died in 1350. Her remains were probably cremated according to Indian custom. It was the Indonesian belief that after death the soul still was tied by earthly bonds to its locale. The idea that the spirit of the newly dead lingered in the vicinity of its place of residence was old Indonesian. After a certain period of

time it was necessary to carry out rituals designed to release the soul so that it could go to whatever the particular conception of paradise was. For Javanese royalty this ceremony occurred twelve years after the death. In 1362, therefore, Rajapatni's soul was released through the ritual of a second cremation and the calling of her spirit into a puppet made of flowers and vegetable matter. The substitute body then was cast away. The actual rites went on in a general atmosphere of feasting and festivities. There are many similarities between ancient Javanese funeral practices and practices elsewhere in the archipelago; the use of puppets as substitute bodies for the spirits of the dead is a particularly common one. The physical remains of the cremation were placed in a stone container which was deposited in the *candi* under the base of the image of the god with whom the newly enshrined ancestor was united. In the case of Rajapatni, she became one with the highest Buddhist goddess, Prajnaparamita.

THE DECLINE OF MAJAPAIT AND THE COMING OF ISLAM

The last century of Majapait's history is very obscure. Wracked by internal struggles and weakened by partition, the country began to disintegrate. Central authority was challenged from the regions. As

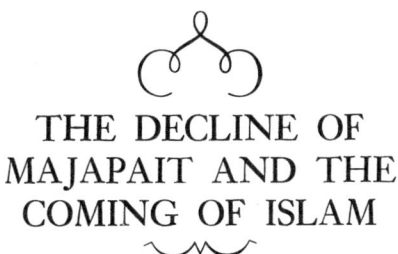

Modern cremation rites in Bali reflect ancient traditions.

decline set in at the political center there was a resurgence of local tradition, particularly a new emphasis on old Indonesian religious beliefs symbolized by the construction of megalithic monuments in the mountains. A second important factor in the decline of the Indianized Javanese state was the coming of Islam. The gradual dominance of Islam probably came about not so much because of a direct confrontation with Majapait (although this is the traditional contention), but rather because of the fact that as the ports of Indonesia came under the control of petty princes converted to Islam, Majapait became increasingly isolated in what was becoming a remote interior of East Java.

In a very general sense Islam spread from west to east in the archipelago. It was brought by Moslem merchants from India, Persia, and the Red Sea countries. The famous European traveler Marco Polo in 1292 had noted the existence of a Moslem country in Northeast Sumatra. Even during its heyday, there were Javanese Moslems living in Majapait—as proved by the existence of Javanese Moslem graves dating from as early as 1376. We can think of the spread of Islam in Indonesia in the same way that we described the process of Indianization. By the end of the fifteenth century nearly all of Sumatra was ruled by Islamic princes—the north coast of Java, and beyond into East Indonesia as far as the island of Mindanao (now Philippine), although probably some kind of Indianized state existed in the interior of East Java until about 1520.

The ending of Indianized political authority on Java did not mean the end of the culture which had been developed around it. On Bali, it was to survive in many forms right up to the present day. On Java, the values and symbols which resulted from the Indo-

Moslem worshippers outside a mosque during Idul Adha (the Feast of Sacrifice). After prayers the faithful will sacrifice cattle.

nesian-Indian cultural amalgam were accepted by the Islamic political authority which succeeded Majapait.

The depth of Islam's penetration into Indonesian culture and civilizations differed throughout the archipelago. Perhaps the locales most thoroughly converted to the teachings of the Prophet Mohammed were the pepper principalities of North Sumatra. They were strongly influenced by the growth of political and economic power in Malacca, the city-state on the west coast of the Malay Peninsula. During the fifteenth century, Malacca, under Moslem rulers, became a great international trading center, monopolizing the trade to and from the archipelago. Ships from all nations called at its harbor. Its population was a mixture of Arabs, Indians, Chinese, Indonesians; Malacca was a polyglot emporium. The Sumatran states of Acheh and Pasai; the Javanese coastal states of Bantam, Tuban, Gresik, etc.; the Buginese from Sulawesi—the "Vikings" of Indonesia; all of these people and many more were represented at Malacca.

On Java, Islamic teaching quickly accommodated itself to the mysticism and speculative philosophy that had developed in the Indianized systems. Moslem teachers of the mystic Sufi order taught ways in which the individual could achieve a personal union with the divine spirit—this was familiar religious territory to the Javanese but they resisted the stale and arid doctrines of Islamic legalists. The later dynastic chronicles of the Moslem courts of Java were analagous to the older legendary and mythic tales in their continued identification of the king with the Hindu god Vishnu and the pervasive presence of the indigenous goddess, Dewi Shri. Even today on Java, although the population is statistically Islamic, the religious world view is still a mixture of animism and Shiva-Buddhism with an overlay of a peculiarly Javanese Islam. It is not uncommon, for example, to encounter on the sites of the *candis* where the kings and queens were enshrined as a Hindu or Buddhist

An ancient ship from the reliefs of Barabodur.

god and goddess, fresh flower and food offerings to local spirits by villagers who, if questioned, would say they were good Moslems. Part of the tension in modern Indonesia between the Javanese and the other Indonesians is a religious tension; the Javanese cling to their own local ways of life and worship in contrast to the universal views of Moslem purists.

THE COMING OF THE EUROPEANS

In the year 1498, the Portuguese explorer, Vasco da Gama, rounded Africa and sailed up its east coast, across the Persian Gulf and on to Calicut in Southern India. Only a few years later, in 1511, the Portuguese made war on Malacca and ended this Malayan port's primacy in the Southeast Asian trade. From their own bases, the Portuguese roamed the Indonesian archipelago with cross and sword in hand, building their own monopoly in the spice and pepper trade. In an effort to break the Portuguese strangle-hold, other European trading companies eventually became active, fighting the Portuguese, local rulers, and among themselves. Nearly a century after Vasco da Gama's arrival in the East, the first Dutch trading ship dropped anchor in the harbor at Bantam, near present day Jakarta, commencing a Dutch-Indonesian relationship which did not end for nearly 350 years—in 1949, the sovereignty of the

One of the many temples in Indonesia where offerings of fresh flowers and food continue to be brought.

Netherlands East Indies was transferred to an independent Indonesian state.

About this period of Dutch imperial and colonial activity in Indonesia it has been said that Indonesian society was viewed from the deck of a European-owned ship, the wall of a Dutch-controlled fort, or the porch of a white colonial's counting-house; the point being that if Indonesia was considered at all it was as an appendage of Europe. The history of Indonesia became the history of the Dutch in Indonesia. We know that indigenous culture and tradition survived. We know that many petty sultanates in the islands had their own, rich local history. We know that for many years the European presence in the archipelago did not transform the basic character of local cultures. In part this was because the relationship was technologically equal and commercial; there was no great cultural superiority. Not only were the Dutch just one of many local powers in the archipelago struggling for influence and trade, but also, for many, many years the Dutch pursued their commercial activities indirectly, through contracts and treaties signed with the local, Indonesian authority. Only gradually did the officials of the Dutch East-India Company push out beyond the walls of their fort at Batavia (now called Jakarta) and take territory themselves.

The Dutch coexisted on Java with the rulers of the new, Moslem Mataram dynasty, whose capital was located in Central Java. Moslem power in Java was, according to traditional history, founded by Raden Patah, a son of the last king of Majapait. The official genealogy of the rulers of Mataram proves the persistence of the legendary symbols of rightful authority on Java. It begins with Adam and his descendants, Hindu gods, the heroes of the *Mahabharata*, mythical kings of Java, the Kadiri king Jayabaya, famous for his prophecies, Panji and his descendants, and the kings of Majapait. On the other hand, the Mataram rulers also traced their descent back through another line to the Moslem saints and prophets, ultimately to Mohammed himself. Although in our eyes these genealogies are patently fictional, they served the purpose in Java

A Dutch general and his staff during a period of war with the Indonesians in 1901.

of proving that the Moslem rulers of the second Mataram were rightful rulers in an unbroken line of succession. The Mataram court was organized along the lines of the traditional Indianized courts. Even the cosmological concept of the court as the symbolic center of the universe was maintained. Court literature reflected the traditions of the past. Court poetry utilized the stories and themes of the great *kekawins* recast in modern Javanese verse and language. The texts on morals and ethics were embedded with the precepts of Indianized Javanese attitudes as opposed to Islam.

Javanese political power was broken by the middle of the eighteenth century. After a series of wars with its neighbors the Mataram kingdom engaged in a civil war which ended with the Dutch imposing a partition of the kingdom between two nobles, one the ruler at Surakarta (Solo) the other at Jogjakarta. Elsewhere in the archipelago the Dutch rule remained largely indirect so long as the required deliveries of agricultural products were made by the local potentates.

MODERN INDONESIA

The modern Indonesian state had its boundaries set by the artificial limits of the colonial Netherlands East Indies regime. Indonesia as a legal or political concept did not exist before modern times. Within the framework of the current Indonesian state, however, is contained a historical sphere of influence that had at its center Java. The ancient rulers of Java termed themselves rulers of "The Whole of the Island of Java as well as Madura and Bali, and All of the Other Islands." As we have already noted, the incorporation of the different peoples of the archipelago within the boundaries of the modern state has produced tensions. There is a definite cultural antagonism which can be defined as Javanese as opposed to the non-Javanese. The tension is heightened by the fact of Javanese population figures. The non-Javanese have an understandable fear that modern Indonesia might become merely a vessel for Javanese expansionism. Indonesian nationalist leaders have sought to avoid the conflict between ethnic-linguistic groups by emphasizing attitudes and symbols which are ethnically neutral.

A good example is language. The largest single linguistic group in Indonesia is the Javanese speaking group. Unlike other countries where there is ethnic plurality, the dominant language (that spoken by the greatest number of people) did not become the national language. In order to prevent the language question from dividing people, nationalist leaders did not choose Javanese but adopted Malay, called *Bahasa Indonesia*, as the language of unity. Rather than the non-Javanese finding themselves in an inferior position with respect to the Javanese, all Indonesians, including the Javanese, have had to learn a language that is native to only a very few Indonesians on one part of the coast of Sumatra. Malayan, however, over the centuries had been an international language in that for many years it had been the language of trade and commerce.

Another example of the way in which the nationalist leaders have sought to reduce ethnic tension is by suggesting that there are common elements linking the different peoples of the archipelago, one to the other. At the most abstract level is a notion of "Indonesian-ness" which suggests that there are common social values underpinning every Indonesian group. Not the least of these is the value placed on cooperative harmony. This is particularly important in decision making. Whereas in the western mode of decision making we have placed great emphasis on one man–one vote (that is to say, every man's right to disagree), the Indonesian stress is on absence of divergent opinion. Indonesians claim to make decisions through a process called *musjawarah-mufakat*—deliberation and consensus. It is felt that this accords with the social

processes traditional to the Indonesian village. Harmony is again displayed through the practice of mutual assistance (*gotong rojong*) in the accomplishment of economic tasks. In fact, that which is "Indonesian" cannot help but acquire a Javanese tinge. Even the late President Sukarno, who for three decades was the living symbol of an Indonesian nationalism, was viewed by the Javanese within the framework of their traditional attitudes toward divine kings.

On a purely cultural level, modern Indonesia encompasses widely disparate peoples. In the jungles of Irian, man still lives in the Stone Age. In East Indonesia, swidden agriculture is practiced. On Nias, an island off the west coast of Sumatra, a megalithic culture still blooms. On Bali, a pale echo of Majapait attracts tourists by the thousands. In the mountains of East Java a group of people, the Tenggerese, still practice corrupted Shiva-Buddhist rituals. The Indonesian national motto is *Bhineka Tunggal Ika* which we can translate as "Unity from Diversity." But, given the differences, how is that unity to be achieved?

We have emphasized as we have sketched the history of ancient Indonesia the way in which foreign cultural influences have been received and converted into something indigenous—the basic continuity of values that lay behind the Indonesian society. Indianization meant on Java the Javanization of Indian forms. Now, however, a new cultural wave is challenging the essential identity of all Indonesians including the Javanese. This is the challenge of modernization conceived as rapid economic and social progress as measured by the yardsticks of European and North American industrial societies. Can the values that gave meaning to life in a basically agricultural society provide the basis for building a modern economy?

Today, Javanese life is not too different in outlook than Javanese life two or ten centuries ago. The prohibitions and taboos as-

Rice fields surround a typical village.

sociated with a view of nature that has little to do with Islam still are observed. The significant occasions in life are marked by *slametans*, the characteristic expression of social identity and cosmic harmony. The typical Javanese probably believes, consciously or subconsciously, in the magical attributes of inanimate objects. A good example of this is Javanese attitudes toward the ceremonial knife, the *kris*. A kris is a wavy-bladed weapon made from a special steel alloy. Each kris is thought to have a soul of its own which can love or hate, be happy or unhappy.

In his home even the most modern Javanese may dress in a traditional fashion, wearing a batik sarong, with ancient Javanese patterns. Batiking is an indigenous craft in which cotton cloth is waxed, a design is inscribed, and then the cloth is dyed. Another area is waxed, a second color of dye used—this process is repeated until all of the design is completed. The Javanese may at some point in his life attach himself to a religious teacher who will impart to him mystical knowledge. He very likely will also consult a soothsayer. He almost certainly will see in the ethics of the *wayang* a guide to his personal life. All in all, his "Javanese-ness" gives him a personal identity that links him to other Javanese and distinguishes him from the non-Javanese. This in a sense is his personal heritage from the past.

There is nothing cultural to prevent the Javanese, or Batak, or Balinese, or member of any of the other many culture groups in modern Indonesia from becoming a doctor, engineer, nuclear physicist, airplane pilot, draftsman, economist, or to preclude his learning any of the other skills necessary for economic growth. There is no need to believe that modernization necessarily has to destroy that part of traditional culture which gives the individual a secure sense of who he is. This certainly was not the case in Japan. "Unity" in terms of all Indonesians sharing in the benefits of expanded

Spirits of dead ancestors in wood and fabric from the island of Nias.

economic development may grow while "diversity" provides a psychological buffer to the strains of social change.

Indonesians have a phrase, *tanah air kita*, "Our earth and sky," to describe their homeland. On that earth, under that sky, man has lived for thousands of years. Kingdoms have come and gone. Wars have been fought; won and lost. Alien visitors have come and gone. Underneath all of the activity recorded in Indonesian history there has been a constant factor: the quality and mode of life in the agricultural village tied closely to the productive energies of nature. This has been the continuity of Indonesian history. It continues to provide a basic framework of stability as Indonesia moves into the future.

Above: A wavy-bladed kris with its scabbard. Each kris is thought to have a soul of its own. Below: A soothsayer in a religious ceremony reflecting the old traditions on Sumatra.

CHRONOLOGY

800–500 B.C.	Coming of the Indonesian peoples.
400–500 A.D.	Earliest inscriptions from Indianized Courts: East Borneo, West Java.
600–700	Growth of Sumatran kingdom of Shrivijaya.
732	Earliest dated inscription from Central Java.
760	Earliest dated inscription from East Java.
760–830	Shailendra kings of Java (Barabodur).
732–900	Sanjaya Dynasty of Central Java (Prambanan).
883	Earliest dated inscription from Bali.
926	Shift of court to East Java.
1016–1017	Destruction of East Javanese court (by Shrivijaya?).
1117–1222	Kadiri Dynasty.
1222–1292	Singasari Dynasty.
1294–1500	Majapait Dynasty.
1300–1500	Growth of Islamic courts in Sumatra.
1400–1500	Development of Islam on north coast of Java.
1511	Destruction of Malacca by Portuguese.
1597	First Dutch trading vessel arrives at Bantam.
1942–1945	Japanese Occupation.
1945	Indonesian Declaration of Independence.
1949	Transfer of Sovereignty from Netherlands to Indonesia.

OTHER BOOKS TO READ

Brandon, James. *On Thrones of Gold: Three Javanese Shadow Plays.* Cambridge: Harvard University Press, 1970.

Holt, Claire. *Art in Indonesia: Continuities and Change.* Ithaca, N.Y.: Cornell University Press, 1967.

Legge, J. D. *Indonesia.* Englewood Cliffs, N.J.: Prentice Hall, 1964.

Peacock, James L. *Indonesia: An Anthropological Perspective.* Pacific Palisades, Calif.: Goodyear Publishing Company, Inc., 1973.

Poole, Frederick King. *Indonesia.* New York: Franklin Watts, 1971.

Smith, Datus C. *Land and People of Indonesia.* Philadelphia: J. B. Lippincott, 1968.

Vlekke, B. H. M. *Nusantara: A History of Indonesia.* The Hague and Bandung: Van Hoeve, 1959.

INDEX

Adi-Buddha, 30
Africa. *See* individual countries.
Agriculture, 2, 73
    Bronze Age, 16, 17
    Middle Stone Age, 12, 13
    New Stone Age, 13, 14
Airlangga, 40
Amazon people, 14
Amir Hamza, 59
Ancestor worship, Bronze Age, 17
Angrok. *See* Ranggah Rajasa.
Animistic culture, 17
Ape-man. *See* Java man.
Archaeologists, 4, 8, 25, 29, 33
Architecture, 26, 29, 33
Arjuna Mountains, 42
Art
    Bronze Age, 17
    Middle Stone Age, 13
Art forms, 23, 25, 42, 50, 51, 54, 56, 70
Asia. *See* individual countries.
Australia, aborigines in, 14

Bali, 1, 17, 23, 40, 43, 50, 62, 70, 73, 74

Bantam, 67
Barabodur monument, 29, 30
Batiking, 74
Bhairava, 45
Bharatayuddha, 23
Bone industry, 12
Borneo. *See* Kalimantan.
Brahma, 26, 30
Brahmans. *See* Hindu religion.
Brantas River, 33, 40, 47
Bronze Age, 16–19
Bronze-Iron Age, 17
Buddhism, 20, 25, 26, 29, 30, 43, 45–47, 48, 61, 64, 73
Burma, 17

Calicut, 67
Cambodia, 29, 50
Candis, 25, 26, 48, 64
Cannibalism
    in Java Man, 9
    in Mesolithic culture, 12
    in Solo Man, 11
Celebes. *See* Sulawesi.
Central Javanese period, 25–33
China, 2, 20, 43, 44
Climate in time of Java Man, 9

(80)

Colonial powers in Indonesia, 2
    See also Dutch in Indonesia
    and Europeans in Indonesia.
Commerce, early Indonesia, 20

Darwin, Charles, 7
Dayak people, 17
Descent lines, 59
Dewi Shri, 47, 53, 64
Domestication of animals
    Middle Stone Age, 12
    New Stone Age, 13
Dongson culture, 16–19
Drama. See Wayang.
Dubois, Eugene, 4, 7
Dutch East India Company. See
    Dutch in Indonesia.
Dutch in Indonesia, 2, 67, 68

East Java. See Java.
Ethnic groups, 2
Europeans in Indonesia, 67–70

Festivals, 53
Fishing, Middle Stone Age, 13
Fossils. See Java Man.
Funan, 29
Funeral rites, 59, 61

Gajah Mada, 50
Geography of Indonesia, 1
Glacier effects, 7

Haematite, use of, 12
Hindu religion, 19, 25, 26, 30, 36,
    40, 42, 47, 48, 64, 68
Historical sources, Javanese, 23,
    25
Hoabinhian sites, 12
Holland, 7
Holocene epoch, 7
Homo erectus, 7
Homo sapiens, 9
Homo solonensis. See Solo Man.
Hunting, Middle Stone Age, 13

I Tsing, 20
India, 2, 20
Indianized states, Indonesia, 19–
    23, 25, 33, 35, 44, 47–53
Indonesia, modern, 1, 2, 4, 70–77
Indonesian islands, 1
Influences of ancient Indonesia,
    70–77
    See also individual cultures,
    empires, and dynasties, *and*
    Religious beliefs and cults.
Irian Barat. See New Guinea.

Jakarta, 19, 67
Java, 1, 2, 4–16, 17, 19, 20, 22,
    23, 25–33, 34–39, 40, 42, 43–
    44, 45–53, 54, 56, 59, 61
    See also individual cultures,
    empires, and dynasties.
Java Man, 4–8

(81)

Java Sea, 1
Javanese historical sources, 23, 25
Javanese society, ancient, 34–39, 45, 47
Jaya Katwang, 43, 44
Jenghis Khan, 44
Jogjakarta, 30, 70

Kadiri dynasty, 40, 42, 43, 44, 68
Kalimantan, 1, 11, 17, 19
Kawi Mountains, 42
Kertanagara, 43, 44, 45, 59
Kubilai Khan, 44
Kutei, 19, 48

Lamaism, 45
Land rights, ancient Indonesia, 35, 36, 39
Languages, 19, 23, 36, 71
Laos, 17
Lesser Sunda islands, 1, 17
Lingas, 25, 26

Madura, 43, 70
Mahabharata, 54, 68
Mahakam River, 19
Mahayanists, 26, 29
Majapait Empire, 2, 25, 39, 44, 45, 47–53, 61, 62, 68, 73
Malacca and Strait of, 1, 20, 64, 67
Malay people and peninsula, 16, 20, 48, 50, 71

Malayu, 43
Marco Polo, 62
Marriage of Arjuna, The, 42
Mataram dynasty, 25, 26, 68, 70
Materials, building, 25, 26
Melanesians, 12–13
Mesolithic culture, 11–13
Metal workers, 16–19
Microliths, 13
Middle Stone Age, 11–13
Mindanao, 22, 62
Mohammed, 64, 68
Moluccas, 1
Mongols, 43, 44
Mulavarman, 19

Nagarakertagama, 25, 48, 51, 59
Natural resources, 2
Neolithic culture, 13–16
New Guinea, 1, 12, 14, 73
New Stone Age, 13–16
Ngawi, 9
Nias, 73
Nobility titles. *See* Javanese society, ancient.
North Vietnam, 12

Old Java Man, 8
Old Javanese, 23
Old Stone Age, 8, 9
Origin of Species (Darwin), 7

Pacific Islands, 12

(82)

Palaeojavanicus, 8
Palaeolithic industry, 9
Palaeolithic period, 8–11
Palaeontologists, 4, 7
Palembang, 20
Panji stories, 48, 50, 56
Papuans, 12
Patjitan industry, 9
Philippines, 1, 11, 22
Pikatan, 30
Pithecantropus erectus, 7, 9
Pleistocene period, 7, 8, 9, 11
Population figures and mixtures, 1, 64, 71
Prajnaparamita, 61
Prehistory, Indonesia, 4–8, 11
Purifying rituals, 47
Purnavarman, 19

Raden Patah, 68
Rajapatni, 59, 61
Rajasanagara, 48, 50
Ramayana, 23, 33, 42, 54
Ranggah Rajasa, 42, 44, 59
Recent epoch. *See* Holocene epoch.
Religious beliefs and cults, 17, 19, 23, 25, 26, 29, 30, 36, 40, 42, 43, 45–47, 48, 61–67
    See also Hindu religion and Buddhism.
Rice, 2, 14, 16, 17, 22
Russia, 2

Sanjaya, 25
Sanskrit, 19, 23, 34, 42
Shailendra dynasty, 26, 29, 30
Shiva, 25, 26, 29, 43
Shivaite culture, 25, 26, 29, 30, 45–47
Shraddha. *See* Funeral Rites.
Shri Laksmi, 47, 48
Shrivijaya culture, 20, 22, 33, 40
Sindok, 33, 40
Singasari dynasty, 39, 40–44, 45
Solo, 30, 70
Solo Man, 9
Solo River, 4, 7, 9, 33
Spice Islands, 1
Stone Ages, 11, 14
    See also Middle Stone Age, New Stone Age, Old Stone Age.
Sufi order, 64
Sukarno, 73
Sulawesi, 1, 12, 17, 22
Sumatra, 1, 11, 12, 17, 20, 22, 43, 62, 64–71
Sumatralith, 12
Sunda, 50
Surakarta. *See* Solo.
Swidden agriculture, 14, 73

Taruma, 19–20
Tenggerese, 73
Thailand, 50
Tibet, 45

Toalean culture, 12, 13
Tools
    Java Man, 8
    Metal, 11, 14, 16, 17
    Middle Stone Age, 12, 13
    New Stone Age, 13, 14
    Solo Man, 9
    Wadjak Man, 11
Toradja people, 17
Trinil, 4, 7

Vasco da Gama, 67
Vietnam, 16

Villages, ancient Indonesia.
    See Javanese society, ancient.
Vishnu. *See* Hindu religion.
Volcanic deposits, 8

Wadjak Man, 9
Wayang, 54, 56
Wijaya, 43, 44
    See also Majapait empire.

Yoga, 45
Yuan dynasty, 44

ABOUT THE AUTHOR

Donald E. Weatherbee is an Associate Professor in the Department of International Studies at the University of South Carolina where he specializes in Southeast Asia. He has worked and traveled extensively in Southeast Asia and has taught at the university in Jogjakarta, Indonesia, where he helped develop the first international relations curriculum in an Indonesian university.

A native of Maine, Dr. Weatherbee was educated at Bates College and holds M.A. and Ph.D. degrees from the Johns Hopkins School of Advanced International Studies. He now lives in Columbia, South Carolina.